"God Pleasing Faith"

Rev. Daniel L. Patrick

Edited By: T.L. Gray

Vabella Publishing

Vabella Publishing
P.O. Box 1052
Carrollton, Georgia 30112

©Copyright 2011 by Daniel L. Patrick

All rights reserved. No part of the book may be reproduced or utilized in any form or by any means without permission in writing from the author. All requests should be addressed to the publisher.

Manufactured in the United States of America

13-digit ISBN 978-0-9834332-5-5

Library of Congress Cataloging-in-Publication Data

Patrick, Daniel L., 1952-
God pleasing faith / Daniel L. Patrick ; edited by T.L. Gray.
p. cm.
ISBN 978-0-9834332-5-5 (pbk.)
1. Christian life--Biblical teaching. I. Gray, T. L. II. Title.
BS2545.C48P377 2011
248.4--dc23
                    2011046759

God Pleasing Faith/Rev. Daniel L. Patrick

Contents

Dedication 5

Forward 7

Introduction 9

God Pleasing Faith is moved with Fear 11

God Pleasing Faith Condemns the World 19

God Pleasing Faith Walks in Faith 33

God Pleasing Faith Declares 41

God Pleasing Faith is Strong Faith 49

God Pleasing Faith Covers Our Children 53

God Pleasing Faith Has a Price 61

God Pleasing Faith Produces 71

Conclusion 81

Dedication

This book is dedicated to my late mother, Marie Elizabeth Patrick. I want to thank her for loving me and never giving up on me. Her prayers, faith and love are the reason I now live a life dedicated to the ministry.

Thanks, Mom.

I miss you!

Forward

I have had the great privilege of knowing Daniel Patrick for over 20 years. Over these past two decades we have developed a deep personal, spiritual and intimate relationship, or should I say the Holy Spirit has blended our lives and ministries together in sweet harmony.

In the scripture God says, "Iron sharpeneth iron; so a man sharpeneth the countenance of a friend." Proverbs 22:17. For the past 20 years this young preacher, now a seasoned Pastor, has been sharpening my spiritual life and honing my own ministry as a Pastor- Teacher in the body of Christ. I am now in my 48th year of preaching God's Word and never have I had a friend so true who is a kindred spirit.

Daniel has developed a keen sense of the presence of God and the moving of the Holy Spirit. I am a better Pastor and Preacher for having known him. You would do well to carefully pray your way through this subject matter of developing "a faith that pleases God". I have been blessed and you will too. Let me caution you: Don't be in a hurry. Meditate on each chapter and allow God to baptize you with its truth.

My prayer is that the Holy Spirit will quicken (the creative life energy force of God) your faith. Walk with your Heavenly Father as He leads you into all the fullness of God as you pursue this study.

Dr. David R. MacDonald
Founding Pastor – Teacher of Abundant Life
Fellowship Ministries
Nashville, Michigan

Introduction

Faith has many facets, and to attempt to exhaust or expose all of them in this book would be absurd. However, my wish is that more revelation of the power of faith be known unto every reader.

May you be richly blessed as you read and study this book on God-Pleasing Faith.

Rev. Daniel L. Patrick

Chapter 1
God Pleasing Faith is moved with Fear

Hebrews 11:6 – "⁶But without faith it is impossible to please him: for he that cometh to God must believe that he is, and that he is a rewarder of them that diligently seek him."

Anyone who comes to God MUST believe that **He** is; and that **He** is a rewarder of those who diligently seek him. Through Scripture we can conclude that to doubt God's Word is to doubt the very existence of God, because God and his Word are one in the same as stated in John 1:1[1]. As Christians, we need to realize this because it is impossible to believe in the existence of God and not believe in the Word of God.

As we study the Scriptures throughout this book, we will uncover the formula, discover the ingredients and find the key to having the kind of faith that pleases God. It is not the size of our need, the desperation of

---

[1] *John 1:1* – *"¹In the beginning was the Word, and the Word was with God, and the Word was God." (KJV)*

our need, or the emotion of our need that moves God; it is faith that moves God.

We Must Heed God's Warning

Hebrews 11:7 – "⁷By faith Noah, being warned of God of things not seen as yet, moved with fear, prepared an ark to the saving of his house;..."(KJV)

It states in this scripture that Noah was warned by God of things not yet seen. Isn't it a blessing to have a God who will tell us of things before they happen? He warns us of things not yet seen in the natural.

We know from the story in Genesis, that God warned Noah of the judgment that was coming; He told Noah to build an ark. In Genesis 6:5-7[2] we learn why; because God saw the wickedness of man. He told Noah that He was going to destroy all flesh. What an interesting statement. Some scholars say this is just a

---

[2] <u>Genesis 6:5-7</u> – *"⁵And God saw that the wickedness of man was great in the earth, and that every imagination of the thoughts of his heart was only evil continually. ⁶And it repented the LORD that he had made man on the earth, and it grieved him at his heart. ⁷And the LORD said, I will destroy man whom I have created from the face of the earth; both man, and beast, and the creeping thing, and the fowls of the air; for it repenteth me that I have made them". (KJV)*

figure of speech, but I find that God to this day still wants to destroy the flesh. He sent Jesus, His only Son to destroy the works of it, and tells us not to walk by it.

In Hebrews 11:7 it says, *"by faith Noah"*. How many know the flesh can be an enemy to our faith?

God told Noah He was going to destroy all flesh. Noah heeded the warning of a judgment to come. As in the days of Noah, there is a judgment coming. The Bible says that we all must appear before the Judgment Seat[3], and that sinners must all appear before the Great White Throne of Judgment[4]. It is not something yet seen, but it is coming.

---

[3] *2 Corinthians 5:10* – *"For we must all appear before the **judgment seat** of Christ; that every one may receive the things done in his body, according to that he hath done, whether it be good or bad." (KJV)*

[4] *Revelation 20:11-15* – *"[11]And I saw a great white throne, and him that sat on it, from whose face the earth and the heaven fled away; and there was found no place for them. [12]And I saw the dead, small and great, stand before God; and the books were opened: and another book was opened, which is the book of life: and the dead were judged out of those things which were written in the books, according to their works. [13]And the sea gave up the dead which were in it; and death and hell delivered up the dead which were in them: and they were judged every man according to their works. [14]And death and hell were cast into the lake of fire. This is the second death. [15]And whosoever was not found written in the book of life was cast into the lake of fire."(KJV)*

God Pleasing Faith/Rev. Daniel L. Patrick

In 2 Corinthians 5:9[5] scripture states we labor to be accepted of Him. Now we must not get this confused with working our way into heaven. Man is not justified by works, but by faith. However, we can't deny what is being said, nor are we to explain it away because we don't think it applies to us. I believe what Paul is trying to say here is, "If you are a Christian, act like it. We must live a life that is acceptable to God."

Now, let's combine this with what we learned in Hebrews 11:7. We see Noah was forewarned of God's judgment.

Noah Was Moved With Fear

Hebrews 11:7 states Noah was moved with fear. We have all but abolished this type of fear the Bible clearly talks about here. In all our teachings in the past concerning faith, how many of them talked about fear?

This scripture could have said, *"By faith, Noah being warned of God of things not yet seen, prepared*

---

[5] *2 Corinthians 5:9* – *"⁹Wherefore we labour, that, whether present or absent, we may be accepted of him." (KJV)*

an ark," but it didn't. It said Noah was moved with fear. **Fear isn't always the evidence of doubt, but it can be the catalyst to engage faith.**

When God told Noah that He was going to bring judgment upon the earth, Noah was moved with fear. Why? It wasn't because he didn't have faith. On the contrary, it was because he did have faith. He knew God was going to do what He said He would do, and that was the way it was going to be.

In the story of Ananias and Sapphira in Acts 5:1-11, we discover that this couple only gave a certain part of what they promised. As we read the rest of this chapter, we find that Ananias and Sapphira died. When Ananias and Sapphira died, great fear came upon all that heard and also the Church; not only the sinner or unbeliever, but the Church. **Sometimes the Church needs to be moved with fear.**

The word *fear* in the Greek means to be afraid or to be frightened. This is the New Testament. This occurrence happened under the covenant in which we currently live.

Noah heeded the warnings of God. He was moved with fear, so he prepared an ark. But, scripture doesn't stop there, because Noah didn't just prepare an ark; he prepared it to the saving of his house.

The ark is symbolic of the safety of God; it means a protective covering or to surround oneself. This is another example of God ordaining the husband to keep a spiritual watch over his house, which we discussed in my last book, *As for Me & My House*. **By Noah's actions, his whole family was saved.**

I can only imagine how Noah was mocked and ridiculed during the long period it took him to build the ark, or how his family was presumably mocked and ridiculed. His wife may have been accused as being crazy for staying with Noah, the children were more than likely encouraged to escape and get free from that religious bondage, and the daughter-in-laws may have second guessed their marriage choices. Only to find that after the flood all that mockery and ridicule was worth their salvation.

Thank God that Noah was a man who believed God enough to be moved with fear to prepare an ark for the saving of his house. Women, can you see how very important it is to marry a God-fearing man?

In order to have the faith Hebrews 11:1 speaks about, we must do what Hebrews 11:7 talks about. Most of the time we cast our confidence away too soon because we think God is not going to move a certain way or we think we're getting too fanatical about God's Word. Let's get fanatical if that is what it takes.

In order for our faith to have life, we must first give our life to the faith. Noah's faith influenced his practice. He not only said he believed God, his actions proved it. This is where we need to be in our Faith. **Faith that doesn't influence our actions is not true faith!**

Chapter 2

God Pleasing Faith Condemns the World

Hebrews 11:7 – "...by the which he condemned the world, and became heir of the righteousness which is by faith." (KJV)

If we want God-pleasing faith, we must have faith that condemns the world. The word **condemn** in the Greek means to judge against or sentence. And the word **world** in the Greek means all that is in the world, its systems, morals and so forth. When Noah obeyed God, he went against logic and reason, the two things the world lives by. He went against the crowd and the majority in order to obey God. When Noah did this, he condemned the world.

This scripture could have said, *"By faith, Noah built an ark and then went on to verse 8."* But God wanted us to see how God-pleasing faith operated. It functions in the realm of the supernatural. It's the substance of things hoped for, the evidence of things not yet seen!

There are Christians who still have un-saved love ones. We Believers must be moved with fear to the point of preparing an ark to the saving of our house while there is still time. God is still warning His people of what has not yet happened.

We have to realize that the condemning of the world as referenced in this scripture is not referring to the people in the world. When Jesus said he didn't come to condemn the world, but to save it in John 3:17[6], He meant the people. In Hebrews 11:7, the word **world** doesn't mean the people, but the systems and the age in which we live. We must condemn that, not people, in order to have God-pleasing faith.

What It Is To Condemn the World?

When we obey God we condemn the world. When we get to the place where we simply believe God and trust him completely, we condemn the world. God-pleasing faith condemns worldly philosophies.

---

[6] *John 3:17* – "*[17]For God sent not his Son into the world to condemn the world; but that the world through him might be saved." (KJV)*

God-pleasing faith condemns the world's systems by:

- Serving God
- Giving to God
- Raising our children according to His Word
- Accepting and loving people regardless of race, creed or color
- Calling sin – sin

By doing this, we become heirs of the righteousness which is by faith.

God-Pleasing Faith is Obedient Faith

Hebrews 11:8-10 – "⁸By faith Abraham, when he was called to go out into a place which he should after receive for an inheritance, obeyed; and he went out, not knowing whither he went.

⁹By faith he sojourned in the land of promise, as in a strange country, dwelling in tabernacles with Isaac and Jacob, the heirs with him of the same promise:

¹⁰For he looked for a city which hath foundations, whose builder and maker is God." (KJV)

Here is another faith Hall-of-Famer! By faith, Abraham went out, he answered the call, and the inheritance was to come after he made the journey. **Sometimes we want to get the inheritance before we obey God.** Remember the story of the Prodigal Son? He wanted his inheritance right away; he didn't want to wait. Why? Because **he** was more interested in what his father had to give than what **he** could do for his father.

God-pleasing faith will obey God's commands without regard of the consequences. Abraham went out not knowing where he was going. We sometimes give God the fifth degree or interrogate Him to get all the specifics. This is not God-pleasing faith. I'm not referring to whether or not God tells us things, but when we know it is God, we should just do it.

How Far has our Faith Taken Us in Obedience?

- Has God ever asked you for something?
- To go to someone?
- Not to go somewhere?
- Did you obey?

With Abraham, maybe the greatest act of obedience was the offering of Isaac. There are two sides of faith; receiving faith and giving faith. If we are not careful, we will walk in an unbalance of the two.

We can major on the use of faith to receive into our lives; that is using it to gain or prosper (which by the way is okay). But, true faith is also giving faith, knowing that we will receive again. God may ask us to give in times of famine. He may also ask us to give what we already have made plans for such as:

- Our time (hunting, fishing, sporting events)
- Our talents (working with children, singing, writing)
- Our finances
- Ourselves (to the works of God)

Can we have faith to receive from God if we don't have faith to give to God? We need to evaluate ourselves and see which we walk in more – faith to receive or faith to say 'yes' when God calls.

Abraham had decisive faith. He didn't argue, have excuses or waiver. He simply obeyed. Faith that doesn't obey isn't God-pleasing faith. No person who walks by faith always knows where God is leading. All we need to know is that God is not going to lead us wrong. His thoughts and attentions toward us are good and never evil. **We should fear missing God and**

His blessings, to the point of following wherever He leads.

Here are some facts to consider about Abraham:

- Abraham never received the inheritance of the Promised Land.

- He never saw a nation of people born of his seed.

- He never owned a piece of land where he could settle.

- He was a sojourner in the country.

- He never saw his son Isaac, nor his grandson Jacob, receive one parcel of land.

- Despite what appeared to be insurmountable odds against the promise ever being fulfilled, he still believed God.

- He believed it so strongly; he taught it and kept it before his son and grandson continually.

God-Pleasing Faith Sojourns In the Land of Promise

In Hebrews 11:9 we learn that by faith Abraham sojourned in the Land of Promise. This scripture doesn't say in the Promised Land, but the Land of Promise. What is the Land of Promise? **It is the land between the promise of the land and the actual Promised Land. It is the journey between what God has promised and the fulfillment of that promise. It's the land where faith dwells. It is the land that holds onto belief. It is the land that kills the flesh and stretches ones character. It is the land between the hope and the evidence. It is the land where Christians sojourn until the promise itself is received.**

Has God promised you something that has not yet happened? If He has, then you are living in the Land of Promise. Glory to God! Without God we just merely exist. But, with God, we live in the Land of Promise; the land rich in the blessings of God; the land where faith is cultivated and doubt is defeated.

The Land of Promise is where trust in God is put to the ultimate test. It's the land where faithful and mature Christians walk, because it's the land where obedience prevails over circumstances.

God Pleasing Faith Sojourns as in a Strange Country

Up to this point we've examined the faith of Noah, faith that heeded the warning of God, faith that allowed him to be moved by fear, and faith that made him prepare an ark for the saving of his household. He expressed a faith that allowed him to turn his back to the things of the world. We can't prepare an ark that will save our house, until we say **no** to the things of the world.

Next we discovered the faith of Abraham, who by faith went out believing God to the point of being obedient. We discovered **it's not possible to believe God and be disobedient**. Abraham went, without knowing where he was going, and his obedience took him into the Land of Promise. Now we are going to take a look at what it means to sojourn in a strange country.

In Hebrews 11:9 the word **sojourns** in the Greek means to reside as a foreigner. The word **strange** in the Greek means another's; not one's own; foreign or hostile.

Jesus said, ***"We are in this world, but not of this world,"*** but do we really know we should live like it? Abraham had left all his wealth and family to go to a place that he was only promised, not somewhere already established and ready for him to move in. But, in his journey through the Land of Promise, he lived his life as a resident in a foreign country; a hostile country.

God-pleasing faith lives as a foreigner in a foreign land. It lives realizing that the Land of Promise may also be a hostile land. Remember, Jesus said not to marvel that the world hates us. Are we counting this world as strange, or are we attached to it and its systems? Do we want to become a citizen of the world, or is our citizenship in another country?

Once we realize we are not of this world but of a much greater kingdom, we are walking by faith. Sickness and poverty are of this world, **but by faith sickness can't dwell in us , and poverty is overridden by faith in God's provision**. When the enemy comes and tries to latch onto us, we can say "No, I'm not eligible to receive this because I'm not a citizen of this country. The country from which I belong doesn't know anything but life and life in abundance." **I** have spiritual immunity; power to resist any and all infections.

Abraham didn't become a permanent resident of this world because he knew it would hinder his travel to the promise. This is how you and I must view our walk by faith. We've got to do more than **know we are just passing through**, we must live like it. Be careful not to get this confused with God not wanting us to have things. God wants to bless us abundantly, but He also may ask us to give it. **We can get so wrapped up in the blessings of God that we take up permanent residence.** This is not God-pleasing faith.

In [7]Genesis 11:31-32 Abraham got comfortable. Abram received his first call from God years before when he dwelt in Ur of Chaldees. But look at what happened, Abram settled into the land of Haran. This is where Isaac and Jacob got their wives and where he

---

[7] <u>Genesis 11:31-32</u> – "[31]And Terah took Abram his son, and Lot the son of Haran his son's son, and Sarai his daughter in law, his son Abram's wife; and they went forth with them from Ur of the Chaldees, to go into the land of Canaan; and they came unto Haran, and dwelt there. [32]And the days of Terah were two hundred and five years: and Terah died in Haran.(KJV)

raised most of his family. It says in Genesis 12:1 - *"¹Now the LORD <u>had said</u> unto Abram, Get thee out of thy country, and from thy kindred, and from thy father's house, unto a land that I will shew thee:" (KJV)*

God HAD SAID, meaning He'd already told Abram once before in the past. Sometimes God has to shake us a little to keep us moving in the right direction. This is where Abraham was told to leave all the things he clung to, his family and possessions and get moving. **Sometimes we can get more attached to the blessing God has given us than God himself.** When we do, this is not God-pleasing faith.

Sometimes we may be called to leave worldly comforts, interests and pleasures. If we are called, we shouldn't hesitate, but just go. This should go without saying - we should only go if we are sure that it is God who is telling us to go.

God-pleasing faith lays hold of blessings. It makes them become present in our lives. The stronger our faith becomes, the more distance we will put between us and the world. If we would do a Bible study of our own, we will find that the people the Bible speaks of as having great faith and are used for our examples are people who walked as strangers in this world. **Until we give our life to the faith, our faith will have no life.**

Chapter 3
God Pleasing Faith Walks in Faith

I want to have faith that is pleasing to God. Maybe I should rephrase that by saying I want to walk in faith that pleases God.

I was praying one day and the Spirit of God spoke to my heart. He said a lot of people walk "**with**" faith, but few walk "**in**" the faith. Now this is not to make anyone feel bad about faith, but it is to encourage us to make sure that we are walking "in" God-pleasing faith.

The scripture found in Hebrews 11:6 makes a powerful statement – *"He who comes to God must believe that He is…"* To believe that God is, is to believe all that He is. **It is possible to know about what God can do, but not trust Him to do it**. To believe God is; is to believe not only that God can, but that He will!

In previous chapters we have taken a look at Noah and his belief and obedience to God. And also Abraham who was sent out to a place in which he knew not and sojourned as in a strange land. We learned this is how we are to be, as a foreigner in a foreign land, knowing that we are of a greater kingdom, one where everything is going great. We need to realize that we are citizens of a greater and more wonderful kingdom.

The more we realize these truths, the more we will walk in peace and understanding. The attack we experienced in America on 9-11 was just like President Bush proclaimed, "A Battle of Good vs. Evil." But even in this there is a peace to be found. At first upon hearing of the attacks, fear tried to grip me, but then the Holy Spirit reminded me that evil will always be present; and the Apostle Paul said that good will always be opposed by evil. I want to remind you that the word **strange** in Hebrews 11:9 means hostile; and that the world we live in can be hostile.

I don't want to downplay the horrible tragedy that happened, nor the innocent lives that were lost, because it could have been anyone of us or a member of our families. But, not only as a nation should we be provoked, we should also be provoked as Christians. To get the Word out even in greater measure than before, and this takes walking and believing and trusting in the Almighty God. **We need the faith that Noah had. We need to walk as Abraham walked, and we need to more than know God can; we must trust that He will.**

Abraham Had His Sights Set

In Hebrews 11:10, the reason Abraham could sojourn as in a strange country was because his aim was on another. You see, you and I have been translated into the kingdom of God's dear Son as stated in Colossians 1:13.[8] **Our sight should be on where we are, not where we used to be.** This is one of our enemies' greatest tactics, to get us to look elsewhere; to trust and believe in things and people instead of walking in faith.

Faith isn't believing in the non-existent. It's believing in the not yet seen. Faith brings into existence that which already exists. We must believe

---

[8] *Colossians 1:13 – "Who hath delivered us from the power of darkness, and hath translated us into the kingdom of his dear Son." (KJV)*

that the things we need already exist. We don't have to believe to make things exist, but we do have to believe for the unseen to be brought into the seen.

***Mark 11:23-24** – "²³For verily I say unto you, That whosoever shall say unto this mountain, Be thou removed, and be thou cast into the sea; and shall not doubt in his heart, but shall believe that those things which he saith shall come to pass; he shall have whatsoever he saith. ²⁴Therefore I say unto you, What things soever ye desire, when ye pray, believe that ye receive them, and ye shall have them." (KJV)*

Jesus spoke this! In His own words He told us that what we say, without doubting, will come to pass. It doesn't say it will be made to exist, but that it will be brought into existence. As long as we look at it as though it doesn't exist, we will never see it.

Hebrews 11:1 – *"Now faith is the substance of things hoped for, the evidence of things not seen." (KJV)* It doesn't say the evidence of things that don't exist, **just what's not seen.**

God Pleasing Faith/Rev. Daniel L. Patrick

What are your needs today? Can you see them as already existing? Because they do! The enemy wants not only for us to believe that these things are impossible for us to have; he wants us to believe that they don't even exist. God has provided everything we will ever need. **Creation is over. Our faith doesn't make God create our answer. Our faith brings into existence what God has already created!**

God-Pleasing Faith Believes That All Things Are Possible

In [9]Hebrews 11:11 – Through faith, Sara herself received strength to conceive seed. Are we getting this yet? The word **conceive** here refers not only to conception, but also giving birth. God-pleasing faith gives strength to conceive.

To some of us, God's promises are only perception and not conception. We are people who have the seed of God in us. We have mountain-moving, abundant life giving, resurrection power packed faith inside of us. It is just waiting to be birthed into the spirit realm to bring back the promises of God that exist in the unseen.

Sometimes we have faith to conceive, but somewhere along the way doubt comes in and our conception is aborted. For instance, when a woman is pregnant she nurtures and cares for that baby as though it already was born. No woman who willfully conceives perceives not to give birth. Although I'm using the

---

[9] <u>Hebrews 11:11</u> – *"[11]Through faith also Sara herself received strength to conceive seed, and was delivered of a child when she was past age, because she judged him faithful who had promised."(KJV)*

God Pleasing Faith/Rev. Daniel L. Patrick

physical aspect of birth, I'm referring to the spiritual. **Doubt will abort spiritual conception.**

Just as a mother eats the right foods, exercises properly and nurtures her unborn baby, we as Christians are to do the same with an unborn promise of God. We need to eat the right spiritual food (the Word), and exercise properly (prayer, praise and quoting the promise), and care for it until it comes.

Just because the promise is yet unborn, doesn't mean we haven't conceived it. Don't allow doubt to abort the promise!

God-pleasing faith believes even when it appears impossible. Sarah and Abraham were past the age of natural conception, but we can never get too old to conceive spiritually. Through faith, Sarah received strength to conceive. **Faith believes even when it's naturally impossible.** Sometimes I think we accept facts over the truth. Sometimes we accept things because of what **we** know about them. If Sarah would have done this, Isaac may not have been born. The realm of faith that we need to walk in is to believe NOTHING is impossible with God. Believing God for what He has promised us can affect nations, and this is a great example!

God is Faithful

Sarah's promise came because she judged God faithful. You and I need to judge God faithful. If He promised us something, He will deliver it. **God never forgets a promise.**

Chapter 4
God Pleasing Faith Declares

Although faith is simple, it is also complex. It has many facets or depths to it. The more we operate in it, the deeper we see it goes. The simplicity of faith is to simply believe, but the complexity of faith is that many things have to work together to activate it.

I know I keep saying this, but it's time we as Christians begin to know that God already has or will, instead of just knowing that He can. It's time that you and I walk **IN** faith, instead of walking **WITH** faith. It's time to use the faith God has given, instead of just having it in our possession.

The people we have studied about in the previous chapters were people that not only knew God could, but they knew that He would. Their belief and trust in God was vividly shown by their obedience to Him. They counted Him faithful.

God Pleasing Faith/Rev. Daniel L. Patrick

Noah did what God asked even when it didn't make natural sense. Abraham left all that he had to go to a place in which he knew not. Sarah, when she was past age, received strength to conceive seed. **She conceived to give birth to what she believed.** It goes on to say because she judged Him faithful who had promised. We need to judge God faithful to what He has promised.

Abraham & Sarah's Faith

In [10]Romans 4:19-21, these passages refer to Abraham's faith. The Bibles says it was not weak faith, that he considered not his own body. Sometimes when we hear the Word of God, we do consider our own bodies.

What this means is that what God promised went past natural, medical science and what Abraham knew about childbirth. When God promised him that

---

[10] *Romans 4:19-21* – *"*[19]*And being not weak in faith, he considered not his own body now dead, when he was about an hundred years old, neither yet the deadness of Sarah's womb:* [20]*He staggered not at the promise of God through unbelief; but was strong in faith, giving glory to God;* [21]*And being fully persuaded that, what he had promised, he was able also to perform"(KJV)*

he was to be a father, **he didn't even consider what he knew about it**. He didn't say, "But, God, I'm past age, I can't do this." Look what else he didn't consider. He didn't consider the deadness of Sarah's womb, either.

God-pleasing faith doesn't consider anything contrary to what God has promised. He didn't stagger at what God said. In the Genesis account, Sarah kind of staggered, but not Abraham. Sometimes we not only stagger at God's promises, they knock us for a loop. Because many times we operate in mountain-moving faith only when there is no mountain to move. We need to learn to judge God faithful. Abraham was fully persuaded at what God had promised and what God was able to perform.

According to Ephesians 3:20 —*"God is able to do exceeding, abundantly, above all that we ask or think." (KJV)* I want you to think about what you need. Think about what you would like to see God perform in your life or the lives of your loved-ones. Now know this; God is able to do exceeding, abundantly above what you just thought about. Become fully persuaded that God is more than enough.

God-Pleasing Faith is a Persuaded Faith

It says in Hebrews 11:13 – ¹³"These all died in faith, not having received the promises, but having seen them afar off, and were persuaded of them, and embraced them, and confessed that they were strangers and pilgrims on the earth." (KJV)

It says here that all died in the faith, not having received the promise. You see, in order to have faith that is persuaded, we must be willing to walk in the supernatural. Although none of these received, they still had a spiritual vision. They had faith that saw into the unseen, and they were persuaded that whether they saw them fulfilled in the natural, they knew their promises existed in the supernatural. Not only were they persuaded, but they embraced their promises. They held onto them regardless of what or how things appeared in the natural.

We can all learn from this example. How many times have we allowed doubt to enter because of what we saw or didn't see in the natural? **We will never** embrace the promises of God until we are persuaded that He is faithful to His promises.

God-Pleasing Faith Declares

In Hebrews 11:14, the word ***declares*** in the Greek means to exhibit in person or declare by words. God-pleasing faith is a faith that not only says, but also does.

We must not only say we are strangers in a foreign land, we must live like it. We need not be mindful of the world or what it has to offer. Whenever you or I take a stand for Christ, we make a declaration or a statement. We say that we aren't going to bow or give into other things. **We not only say we are separated from the things of this world, but we separate ourselves from them.**

According to the scripture in [11]Colossians 3, we need to seek those things which are above. We need to

---

[11] Colossians 3:1-3 – *"¹If ye then be risen with Christ, seek those things which are above, where Christ sitteth on the right hand of God. ²Set your affection on things above, not on things on the earth. ³For ye are dead, and your life is hid with Christ in God." (KJV)*

set our affections on things above and not on things on the earth. We are foreigners in a strange land. We are dead, and our lives are hid with Christ. We must declare this in the biblical sense. I mean, not only say we are not of this world, but we must also set our affections on the things which are above.

God-pleasing faith takes pleasure in the things of God. God-pleasing faith reckons itself dead to the things of the world.

So, what is it to be hid with Christ in God?

- It is to seek those things which are above where Christ dwells.
- It is to set aside time in our day for reading, praying and communing with God.
- It is to have ongoing communication with God throughout the day.
- It is to know that no matter what the day brings, God will see us through it.
- It is to be hid from the troubles of this world.

- It is to know that no matter what happens in this world, we are hid with Christ.

Now, in [12]Hebrews 11:15 we see the importance of denying this world. If they had been mindful of the country they had left, they may have had opportunity to return. We can't even entertain thoughts about what we could have had or what we could have been, or what we 'gave up' to be a Christian. We can't have the best of both worlds, so to speak.

However, I didn't say that we couldn't be blessed greatly while in this world, but we can't strive to have the best of both lands (countries). We must realize that the country we have been translated into, has everything we could ever need and more.

God is not an additive to what we already have. He is not something we bring into our lives to make it run smoother. He is someone to whom we give our lives to, because when God becomes our life, there may be some things we need to leave behind. We can't even be

---

[12] Hebrews 11:15 – "15And truly, if they had been mindful of that country from whence they came out, they might have had opportunity to have returned." (KJV)

God Pleasing Faith/Rev. Daniel L. Patrick

mindful of our prior life, because if we do, we may just return to it.

Desire the Better Country

We must desire the better country. We must set our affections on the things above, and not on the things of this world. We must be persuaded that God is faithful to fulfill His promises. And we must embrace the promises and confess we are strangers in a foreign land.

Chapter 5

God Pleasing Faith is Strong Faith

In [13]1 Peter 1:6-7 it says that the trial of your faith is precious, and not only precious, but much more precious than of gold that perish.

Although God will never tempt us, He will try us. The word ***tried*** in the Greek means to test; scrutinize, discipline or prove. God-pleasing faith is a faith that is tested. What good would faith be if it wasn't put to the test? **Faith that is tried is faith that is proven.**

You and I are going to go 'through' things in our life. Sometimes these things are going to be hard. But, they are there to make us stronger. **Trials that come into our lives will prove our faith.** They will also reveal the strength of our faith.

---

[13] *1 Peter 1:6-7* – "⁶*Wherein ye greatly rejoice, though now for a season, if need be, ye are in heaviness through manifold temptations:* ⁷*That the trial of your faith, being much more precious than of gold that perisheth, though it be tried with fire, might be found unto praise and honour and glory at the appearing of Jesus Christ:" (KJV*

[14]James 1:2-3 are very familiar passages of scripture, but sometimes we fail to see how valuable they are. Peter told us to greatly rejoice and James tells us to count it all joy. **But when we are in these times we don't really see them for what they are.**

Allow me to interject something here. God doesn't make us sick to test our faith in healing. God doesn't make us poor to prove our faith in His provision, however our faith **is** proven in these times.

God-Pleasing Faith Gives What God Asks

In Genesis 22:1-2 God asked Abraham to offer Isaac. **God-pleasing faith gives God what He asks no matter how valuable it is.** Now we must understand that Abraham had a close relationship with God. He knew it was God asking or telling him what to do. **Abraham didn't offer Isaac on a whim; he remembered God's promises in reference to Isaac.**

---

[14] *James 1:2-3* – *"²My brethren, count it all joy when ye fall into divers temptations; ³Knowing this, that the trying of your faith worketh patience." (KJV)*

In [15]Hebrews 11:18-19 – Abraham remembered what God had promised. Isaac was only a lad, a child at the time God asked Abraham for him, and he knew that the promise of Isaac's seed wasn't fulfilled yet. In verse 19, Abraham accounted (reckoned and concluded) that God was able. It says here that Abraham had faith enough to believe God to raise Isaac up again in order to fulfill His promise. To do this took full persuasion and strong faith.

You and I must come to the place that we are persuaded that if God asks for it, He **will** return more than what we gave. Here is another example of the giving side of faith. Abraham's faith in God was tested. **He was asked to give something that was so valuable to him, and by willing to do so, God gave back more than what Abraham could have imagined.**

It is possible to get caught up and use our faith to receive more than to give. It's the giving side of faith that has to be proven. Jesus said it is more blessed to

---

[15] _Hebrews 11:18-19_ – "[18]*Of whom it was said, That in Isaac shall thy seed be called: [19]Accounting that God was able to raise him up, even from the dead; from whence also he received him in a figure*" (KJV)

give than to receive. **God pleasing faith operates on the principle that it receives back more than it gives.**

What Does God Ask of Us?

Thank God, He doesn't ask for our sons and daughters to be offered as a sacrifice, but He does still ask that we **offer** our sons and daughters to be used of Him.

God asks for our time, talents, money & our whole hearts.

There is no way we will give God what He asks for until we are fully persuaded that He will give back a whole lot more in return. **God-pleasing faith offers what He asks.**

Chapter 6

God Pleasing Faith Covers Our Children

In [16]Hebrews 11:20-22 we see the kind of parents God wants us to be. We see the kind of faith that parents need to please God in reference to their children. I'll be the first to admit that the atmosphere in which we have to raise children today differs from when my children were young. But, I'll also admit that the principles of raising a child with God-pleasing faith haven't changed. As we look at this scripture, we will find many of the things that Moses' parents faced at that time, we still face today. I believe that there is a reason for this scripture to be penned in the context it was written.

---

[16] *Hebrews 11:20-22 –" [20]By faith Isaac blessed Jacob and Esau concerning things to come. [21]By faith Jacob, when he was a dying, blessed both the sons of Joseph; and worshipped, leaning upon the top of his staff. [22]By faith Joseph, when he died, made mention of the departing of the children of Israel; and gave commandment concerning his bones." (KJV)*

Let's set the scene here to make this verse relevant to where we are today!

The Setting

The Growth of Israel

After Joseph, Jacob and his sons settled in the Land of Goshen, Egypt where the Israelites began to grow in number. The new king was threatened by them. **Keep in mind that Egypt represents sin and bondage.** The word ***king*** denotes a kingdom. You can't be rightly called a king unless you rule a kingdom.

So, if Egypt represents sin and bondage, then the king here represents the one who rules over sin and bondage. Who rules over sin and bondage today? Satan.

When God's people begin to increase in number it still makes the king of this world nervous. So, the king of Egypt took the step and tried enslaving Israel into thinking that they would quit multiplying. But, it didn't work. Israel kept reproducing at a rapid pace.

The king then decided to make another try. In [17]Exodus 1:21-22 the king made a law to kill all the male children at birth. Satan hasn't changed; his desire to kill is still active. However, it's not just the males he is after.

Sometimes we can get lax in our parental duties when it comes to protecting our children from the enemy. Satan hasn't changed; he still wants our children, but the method of getting them has many faces.

We as parents must be aware of this, do the same thing Moses' parents did.

What Moses' Parents Did

Hebrews 11:23 – "²³By faith Moses, when he was born, was hid three months of his parents, because they saw he was a proper child; and they were not afraid of the king's commandment." (KJV)

---

[17] Exodus 1:21-22 – "²¹And it came to pass, because the midwives feared God, that he made them houses. ²²And Pharaoh charged all his people, saying, Every son that is born ye shall cast into the river, and every daughter ye shall save alive." (KJV)

It was by faith that his parents did what they did; hide Moses. The word **hid** in the Greek means to conceal; putting proper cover over. Are you getting this? Parents, we are the spiritual covering for our children, and it's our duty to hide our children from the king of this world. We must do whatever it takes to cover them from harm.

In[18] Proverbs 22:6 it says to train up a child. We usually interpret this as just teaching them in word or telling them what they should do. But the word **train** here in Hebrew means to hedge in, to make narrow the way. This means to guide them in the way they should go.

When my grandbabies were little, they sometimes wanted to go places they shouldn't, so I blocked their way. Sometimes they tried to poke their heads through my legs or cried out in stubbornness or defiance, but I couldn't allow their behavior to stop me. I had to hedge them in.

The word **train** also is in reference to a trainer in boxing. This trainer doesn't just leave a post-it-note

---

[18] *Proverbs 22:6 – "⁶Train up a child in the way he should go: and when he is old, he will not depart from it." (KJV)*

God Pleasing Faith/Rev. Daniel L. Patrick

around for the boxer to follow. He doesn't just tell the boxer to set the alarm for 4 am and go run ten miles. No, the trainer gets up with the boxer and makes the run with him all the while telling him of why he is doing it.

You see, parental God-pleasing faith doesn't just leave a post-it-note for the children to:

- Pray
- Read the Word
- Go to church

No, it prays with the child, it reads the Word with the child, it goes to church with the child, and it hides the child from the king of this world.

We need to stay involved in our children's spiritual life as we do their secular one. We go to great lengths to provide for our children's secular education and provisions. We should do even more for their spiritual education. We are to hide (hedge in or make the way narrow) our children. We are to quickly cut them off from any and all danger or wrong doing.

The Reason for Hiding Moses

Also in Hebrews 11:23 we discover that Moses was hid for three months. Why? Because they knew he was a proper child. **Not only did Moses' parents know that the king wanted to kill all male children, they knew that God had a plan for his life.**

As parents, we need to recognize that Satan wants our children, but also and more importantly, God has a plan for their lives. This is why we should hedge them in or hide them.

Moses' parents were not afraid of the king's commandments. We can't allow the enemy to intimidate us, or give into his tactics and lies. As we read Hebrews 11:23 we discovered that Moses' parents had a fearless faith. They knew not to obey the law of the land when it was in opposition to the law of God.

Sometimes we can compromise with our children because we're afraid of what people may think. **God-pleasing faith raises a child according to**

God's plan. God-pleasing faith hides children from the king of this world.

Parental Duty

Get involved, and stay involved in your child's life. Not to the point of provoking them to anger, but know that by being a parent sometimes you're going to make them angry. Be sensitive to how far you go with your child, but you must realize that God has a plan for them. It's the enemy's job to keep them from that plan. Let's be the covering our children need. This is faith that pleases God.

Chapter 7
God Pleasing Faith Has a Price

Hebrews 11:24-27 —" ²⁴By faith Moses, when he was come to years, refused to be called the son of Pharaoh's daughter;

²⁵Choosing rather to suffer affliction with the people of God, than to enjoy the pleasures of sin for a season;

²⁶Esteeming the reproach of Christ greater riches than the treasures in Egypt: for he had respect unto the recompence of the reward.

²⁷By faith he forsook Egypt, not fearing the wrath of the king: for he endured, as seeing him who is invisible." (KJV)

Here in these scriptures lay the description of every born again person. Here is where the rubber meets the road so to speak. What does it really mean to follow Christ? What does it require to please God? What is it to have God-pleasing faith when it comes to following Christ?

There are a lot of doctrines concerning this part of scripture. The call to Christ and living the Christian life is not as easy as some think or teach. In these scriptures, we see that there is a choice to be made, a reproach to be esteemed, a forsaking to be done, a fear to be abolished, and an endurance to be experienced. Following Christ is God-pleasing faith; it is one of love, joy and peace, not only a call to a life of ease, comfort and plenty. It is not only to physical and material prosperity, but to a spiritual prosperity.

We must keep the doctrines of the Bible in balance. We can't major on any one specific. We are to live by every word that proceeds out of the mouth of God.

If there would be a general teaching or preaching that I do, it would be to equip the Saints for the work of the ministry or to help us live the life. To help us understand the trying times of life and realize that they will come. Although we, through Christ, don't have to fight **for** the victory, there are times when we will have to stand **in** the victory.

We were designed by our God to go through things, not stay in them. In [19]John 16:33, Jesus said in the world we would have tribulations. He didn't say in the world there would be tribulation and it will not affect you. He said we would have tribulations, but to be of good cheer, because He has overcome the world. We need to keep this truth in balance, and not only this teaching but all the teachings in the Bible.

Do I believe in prosperity? Do I believe in healing? Do I believe in deliverance? Do I believe in the gifts of the Spirit? Absolutely! But not to the place that they're the reason I follow Christ.

I am persuaded that if I follow Christ in the manner which pleases God, prosperity will be there, healing will come, deliverance will happen, and the gifts of the Spirit will operate. Although the gift of salvation has been purchased by the blood of Christ, there is a cost of being a Christian.

---

[19] *John 16:33* – "*[33]These things I have spoken unto you, that in me ye might have peace. In the world ye shall have tribulation: but be of good cheer; I have overcome the world." (KJV)*

God-Pleasing Faith Refuses

- Refuses to be called anything but Christian

- Refuses to join itself to anything or anyone who is against God

- Refuses to attach itself to the world no matter how good it seems

We must remember that Moses was raised as a child of Pharaoh's daughter. He was raised as a prince in Pharaoh's court. By tradition, Moses was heir to the throne of Egypt. Moses had everything a person could want, even by today's standards. He had:

- Education and knowledge

- Fame & wealth

- Possessions & authority

- Position

- Purpose & responsibility

- All the provisions anyone could possibly need

But, he refused all this! He wouldn't compromise his faith for any of this. When the world dangles a carrot in front of us, we must be sure that it won't cause us to compromise in any way. If it will or does, refuse it. God-pleasing faith says, "No thanks". God-pleasing faith refuses to be called anything but a follower of Christ.

God-Pleasing Faith Chooses Godly Suffering Over the Pleasure of Sin for a Season

Hebrews 11:25 – "25Choosing rather to suffer affliction with the people of God, than to enjoy the pleasures of sin for a season;" (KJV)

Was Moses going to be identified with the Egyptians, or was he going to identify with the people of God?

This is a choice that every person born into this world must make. Do we want to be identified with Egypt (sin & bondage) and all it represents, or do we want to identify with the people of God?

Moses had to choose between the pleasures of Egypt, or pursue God and His promises. Now here again we weren't called to a life of suffering. A Christian's life isn't full of suffering, but when we take a stand for God there will be some unpleasant times. Like Moses, we have a choice – either to go with the crowd or take a stand – either to accept what the world has to offer or offer ourselves unto God.

Moses could have just kept his mouth shut, but he made the right choice. He chose to be identified with God and **all** that entailed, rather than be accepted by Egypt. If we, as Christians, seem to fit into a lot of worldly things, we better check to see how bright our light is shining. If people who don't know Christ are real comfortable around us, we better take a good look at where we are. Not only should unbelievers feel uncomfortable around us, we too ought to feel a little out of place around them.

God-Pleasing Faith Esteems the Reproach of Christ as a Great Treasure

Hebrews 11:26 – "26Esteeming the reproach of Christ greater riches than the treasures in Egypt: for he had respect unto the recompense of the reward." (KJV)

The reason Moses made the choice to suffer with the people of God, is because he esteemed the reproach of Christ greater riches and had respect unto the recompense of the reward.

In order to make Godly choices in life, we must esteem the reproach of Christ greater. To esteem means to deem or judge, and reproach means to taunt or ridicule.

Let me tell you, when we make Godly choices, when we take a stand for Christ, we will be taunted and ridiculed by the world. We must deem or judge this ridicule and taunting as greater riches. Greater riches than:

- To fit in

- To be liked

- To be popular

- To gain social status

- To be invited to 'the' event

- To get on a squad or team

Sometimes esteeming the reproach of Christ will cause us to lose the so-called riches of the world. Sometimes, esteeming the reproach of Christ greater riches will cause us:

- To feel like we don't belong

- To create enemies

- To be unpopular

- To **not** have social status

- To **not** be invited many places

- To **not** be asked to get on the squad or team

It's what we esteem to be the greater. God-pleasing faith will esteem the reproach of Christ, greater riches than what the world has to offer.

Moses esteemed the reproach of Christ greater than the treasures of Egypt because he had respect unto the recompense of the reward. Let's look at this for a moment. The word ***respect*** means to look away from everything else; to intently regard. The reason Moses esteemed the reproach of Christ greater is because he looked away from everything else and intently regarded Christ and all that He is.

By faith, Moses forsook Egypt. When we take a stand for Jesus, we will have to forsake Egypt. We can't fear or allow fear to come upon us no matter what consequences we may face when following Christ. At times it will take courage to go against the majority. At times it will take courage to do what is right instead of what others may want us to do.

I heard a song on the radio and it listed all the things that made us look like or identified us as

Christians such as: fish emblems on our cars, bracelets that read WWJD, bumper stickers and so on. But then it asked, "What about the change; what about the difference?" Is there a distinct difference in us?

God-pleasing faith refuses to be named among anything but Jesus. It chooses the affliction of God's people over the pleasure of sin for a season. It esteems the reproach of Christ greater riches than the treasures of Egypt. In order to walk in Hebrews 11:1 faith, we must do what God-pleasing faith requires.

Chapter 8
God Pleasing Faith Produces

Let's examine the fruit of what God-pleasing faith produces. We all want to have faith that moves mountains, opens blind eyes and sets captives free, but faith is more than this. It's obedience to God when it doesn't look like things are going to work out. It's giving what God requires even when we don't think we have it to give. **It's faith that produces faithfulness** regardless of what we think we have to give up.

Having and walking in God-pleasing faith will produce faithfulness to God. It's being in total surrender to God. It's more than just having bouts of being faithful; it's living a life of faithfulness.

I believe one of the reasons for the examples of Moses, Noah, Abraham & Sarah are to make us aware of the faith they walked in and not just talked about. These people only walked in the promise of the Savior, while we walk in the promises our Savior died to give to us.

The kind of faith you and I need to walk in is the kind that does when asked, and goes where and when it's told to go. It's the kind of faith that is moved with fear to the preparing of an ark for the saving of our household. It's the kind of faith that sojourns in the Land of Promise as in a strange country. It's the kind of faith that receives strength to conceive seed, even when it goes past our physical capabilities. It's the kind of faith that receives promises that are far off and is persuaded of them and embraces them no matter what it may appear.

This kind of faith hides its children, because of God's plan for their lives. It's a faith that refuses, chooses, esteems, forsakes and endures. When we walk in this kind of faith, miracles happen, doors are opened, and God is glorified.

God-Pleasing Faith Produces Supernatural Passage

Hebrews 11:29 – " ^{29} ***By faith they passed through the Red sea as by dry land: which the Egyptians assaying to do were drowned." (KJV)***

Wow, God-pleasing faith passes through things as though they don't even exist! Are we getting this yet? They passed through the sea as if on dry land. And it passes us through places where the devil and his imps will get overtaken. I don't know about you, but I desire to walk in this kind of faith. It will take us through things that would naturally overtake us.

God-Pleasing Faith Makes Walls Fall Down in Our Lives

Hebrews 11:30 – "By faith the walls of Jericho fell down, after they were compassed about seven days." (KJV)

God Pleasing Faith/Rev. Daniel L. Patrick

These walls fell down after they had been compassed about seven days. As we read about this account in the book of Joshua chapter 6, we see that God gave specific instructions before the wall fell down. They were to walk about the wall once a day for six days. Then, on the seventh day, they were to walk around the wall seven times, and on the seventh time they were to blow a ram's horn and all the people were to shout. God-pleasing faith stands strong in the promises of God. Let's read about this account.

Joshua 6:1-5 – "1Now Jericho was straitly shut up because of the children of Israel: none went out, and none came in.

2And the LORD said unto Joshua, See, I have given into thine hand Jericho, and the king thereof, and the mighty men of valour.

3And ye shall compass the city, all ye men of war, and go round about the city once. Thus shalt thou do six days.

4And seven priests shall bear before the ark seven trumpets of rams' horns: and the seventh

day ye shall compass the city seven times, and the priests shall blow with the trumpets.

5And it shall come to pass, that when they make a long blast with the ram's horn, and when ye hear the sound of the trumpet, all the people shall shout with a great shout; and the wall of the city shall fall down flat, and the people shall ascend up every man straight before him." (KJV)

God told Joshua in verse 2, *"I have given you."* Even though God had given Joshua Jericho, he still had to do something. **Sometimes faith demands faithfulness.** Isn't this the common denominator in the examples of faith in Hebrews 11? Isn't the Word of God saying by faith they remained or were faithful?

God could have said, "Joshua when you get up in the morning the wall will be gone", but He didn't. God promised and then demanded faithfulness and obedience. **True faith will produce faithfulness!**

God-Pleasing Faith Is Full of Power

Hebrews 11:32 – "32And what shall I more say? for the time would fail me to tell of Gedeon, and of Barak, and of Samson, and of Jephthae; of David also, and Samuel, and of the prophets:" (KJV)

This is a call to remembrance. Sometimes we need a call to remembrance, we need to be reminded of what power and reward faith has. These men dared to believe God against unbelievable odds, but in every case their faith and faithfulness won them victory. Sometimes our enemy wants us to believe that these are days gone by, that this faith only existed back then, when we have this faith available to us through Christ. **NOW!**

God-Pleasing Faith Subdues Kingdoms

Hebrews 11:33 – "Who through faith subdued kingdoms, wrought righteousness, obtained promises, stopped the mouths of lions." (KJV)

The word **subdue** means to overcome, and the word **kingdom** is in reference to realms. So, we have overcome the spiritual realm of darkness. God has given us victory over all our enemy's devices and tactics. Do you have any kingdoms that need subdued? **God-pleasing faith overcomes all of them!**

God-pleasing faith also:

- Wrought righteousness or works righteousness in us

- Obtains promises – believes God no matter what it may look like

- Stops the mouths of lions – Satan goes around as a roaring lion but faith stops his mouth in our lives

Hebrews 11:34 – "34Quenched the violence of fire, escaped the edge of the sword, out of weakness were made strong, waxed valiant in fight, turned to flight the armies of the aliens." (KJV)

The word **_quenched_** means to put out or extinguish. The word **_violence_** here refers to strength or ability. Essentially what this scripture is saying is that God-pleasing faith will put out or extinguish the strength or ability of the fire, or enemy. **Hallelujah!**

One thing we get mixed up is, we think it takes the fire way. No, but it does take the sting, or the ability of it away. The fire may still be there, but faith keeps it from harming us.

God-pleasing faith also:

- Escapes the edge of the sword, the weapons of our enemies. Again, it may not take the sword away, but it causes us to escape it.

- It makes weakness strong.

- It makes us valiant in war as a mighty soldier.

- It causes armies of enemies to flee.

Getting it yet?

God-pleasing faith or faith that pleases God endures no matter what the circumstance.

The Bible says in Matthew 24:14 that he that endures to the end shall be saved. Up to this point in the book we have read about prominent leaders and people such as Noah, Moses, Abraham and Sarah, but in these verses it doesn't make a specific reference. It's talking about men & women in general, ones who held onto and had God-pleasing faith.

These people were tortured, stoned, sawed in half, put on trial, scourged, imprisoned, tempted, slain with the sword, made to wander about in animal skins without anything; they were afflicted and tortured, but still believed God.

You and I desire mountain-moving, demon-casting- miracle-working faith. We desire faith that pleases God, but what we tend to overlook at times is; God-pleasing faith is also a faith that will have to endure. These men and women endured the testing of their faith; they held onto God and His promises.

God Pleasing Faith/Rev. Daniel L. Patrick

The same God of Noah, Abraham, Sarah and Moses, is the same God today and forever. Set yourself to seek Him.

God Bless!

Conclusion

I pray this book has helped you see faith in a broader sense, and that you continue to walk in God-pleasing faith. **Remember, our faith can't have life until we give our lives to The Faith.**

God Bless!

Rev. Daniel L. Patrick

www.ingramcontent.com/pod-product-compliance
Lightning Source LLC
Chambersburg PA
CBHW072026060426
42449CB00035B/2880